Contents

Welcome to Canada!

Hello! My name's Benjamin Blog and this is Barko Polo, my **inquisitive** dog. (He's named after ancient ace explorer, **Marco Polo**.) We have just got back from our latest adventure – exploring Canada. We put this book together from some of the blog posts we wrote on the way.

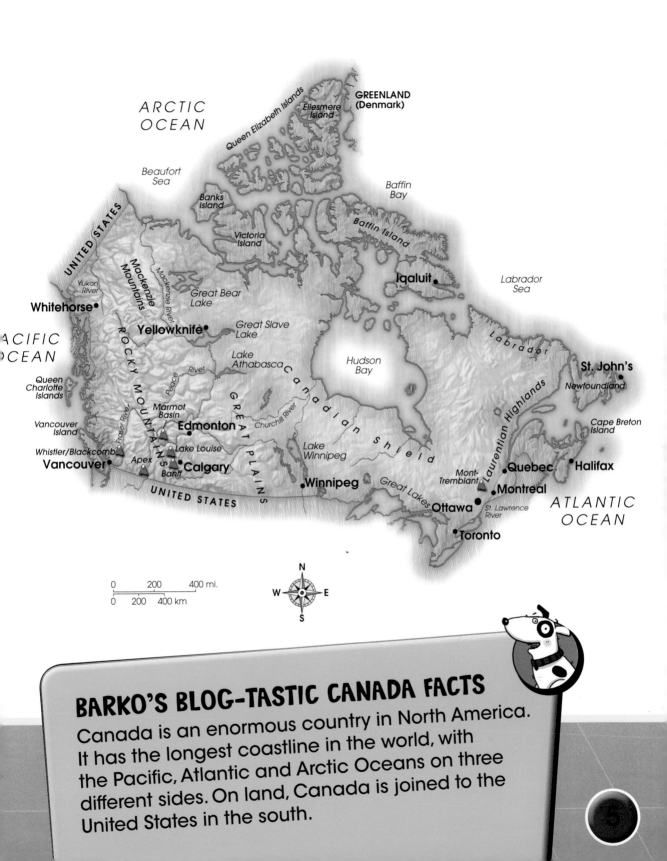

ARCTIC
OCEAN

GREENLAND
(Denmark)

Queen Elizabeth Islands

Ellesmere
Island

Beaufort
Sea

Baffin
Bay

Banks
Island

Baffin Island

Victoria
Island

Mackenzie Mountains

Mackenzie River

Great Bear
Lake

Iqaluit

Labrador
Sea

Yukon
River

Whitehorse

Yellowknife

Great Slave
Lake

PACIFIC
OCEAN

ROCKY MOUNTAINS

Lake
Athabasca

Peace River

Hudson
Bay

Canadian Shield

Labrador

St. John's
Newfoundland

Queen
Charlotte
Islands

GREAT PLAINS

Churchill River

Laurentian Highlands

Cape Breton
Island

Vancouver
Island

Marmot
Basin

Edmonton

Lake
Winnipeg

Whistler/Blackcomb
Vancouver

Lake Louise
Apex
Banff

Calgary

Quebec
Halifax

Mont-
Tremblant
Montreal

Winnipeg

Great Lakes

Ottawa

St. Lawrence
River

ATLANTIC
OCEAN

UNITED STATES

Toronto

0   200   400 mi.

0   200   400 km

N
W   E
S

BARKO'S BLOG-TASTIC CANADA FACTS
Canada is an enormous country in North America.
It has the longest coastline in the world, with
the Pacific, Atlantic and Arctic Oceans on three
different sides. On land, Canada is joined to the
United States in the south.

5

Vikings and Inuits

Posted by: Ben Blog | 17 March at 3.15 p.m.

Our first day in Canada and I've come to L'Anse aux Meadows on the northern tip of Newfoundland. This is where the **Viking** Leif Ericsson landed in around AD 1000. He was the first European to reach North America. I'm off to explore this Viking town.

BARKO'S BLOG-TASTIC CANADA FACTS

This is Iqaluit, the capital of Nunavut (a huge area in the far north of Canada). In 1999, the land was officially given to the **Inuit** people who had lived there for thousands of years. The name *Nunavut* means "our land" in the Inuit language.

Lakes, mountains and islands

Posted by: Ben Blog | 4 April at 9.31 a.m.

From Newfoundland, we headed to Lake Superior. At 82,100 square kilometres (31,700 square miles), it's the world's biggest freshwater lake. You can see how it got its name! It's one of the five Great Lakes on the border with the United States. The others are Michigan, Huron, Erie and Ontario.

BARKO'S BLOG-TASTIC CANADA FACTS

Mount Logan stands 5,959 metres (19,551 feet) tall and is the highest mountain in Canada. To climb it, you have to fly to one of the **glaciers** at the base of the mountain. Then it's a 30-kilometre (19-mile) hike to the top.

Next stop was Baffin Island, back in Nunavut. Huge parts of northern Canada lie in the Arctic Circle and are covered in ice and snow for most of the year. Luckily, the **Inuit** are experts at surviving. They wear pairs of mukluks (sealskin boots) to keep their feet warm.

BARKO'S BLOG-TASTIC CANADA FACTS

Normally, polar bears in Hudson Bay hunt for seals on the sea ice. But if there isn't much food, they sometimes wander into the town of Churchill and **scavenge** in people's rubbish bins.

City sights

Posted by: Ben Blog | 6 May at 2.11 p.m.

Today, we arrived in Toronto, the biggest city in Canada, and headed straight to the CN Tower. At 553 metres (1,815 feet) high, it's one of the tallest towers in the world. You can walk around the outside of the tower, on a ledge near the top. Very scary!

Stanley Park is in the city of Vancouver. Visitors can walk, run or cycle along the Seawall, a path overlooking the Pacific Ocean. Then, if you're feeling tired, you can hitch a lift on the miniature railway.

People of Canada

Posted by: Ben Blog | 18 May at 6.19 p.m.

The **Inuit** and First Nations people have lived in Canada for thousands of years. These people are Haida, a group of First Nations people from British Columbia in the north-west. Many Canadians today are **descended from** settlers who came from Britain and France.

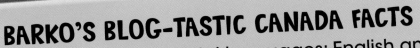

BARKO'S BLOG-TASTIC CANADA FACTS

Canada has two official languages: English and French. French is mostly spoken in Québec. The First Nations and Inuit people also have their own languages. This street sign is in English and French.

ARRÊT
STOP

ARRÊT

ARRÊT

ARRÊT

ARRÊT

Children in Canada start school at the age of five or six and stay until they are 16 or 18. Afterwards, some carry on their studies at college or university. Most subjects are taught in English, but in Québec, there are also many French-language schools.

BARKO'S BLOG-TASTIC CANADA FACTS

In Nunavut, houses have to be built on stilts. They cannot be built straight on the frozen ground. Otherwise, the heat from the houses would melt the ice and the houses would sink.

We're here on Vancouver Island with the Kwakwaka'wakw people. Traditionally, they catch salmon for food. Every year, they hold a special ceremony to say thank you to the salmon. There's a Salmon Dance and a feast, with plenty of salmon to eat, of course.

Feeling hungry

Posted by: Ben Blog | 28 August at 5 p.m.

After another hard day's sightseeing, we stopped for a quick bite to eat. There was plenty to choose from on the menu, but I decided to give poutine a try. It's made of chips, topped with cheese curds and gravy. You can eat it with chicken or bacon, or even lobster.

Canada is famous for maple syrup, which is made from the **sap** of maple trees. The syrup is delicious mixed into porridge, but I like it on pancakes best.

Ice hockey and stampedes

Posted by: Ben Blog | 12 November at 1.10 p.m.

Stopping off in Montreal, we got tickets for an ice hockey game. Ice hockey is fast and furious, and it's the most popular winter sport in Canada, with an ice rink in every town. We're here to watch the Montreal Canadiens, one of the top teams in the country.

BLOG-TASTIC CANADA FACTS

Every year, in July, more than a million people flock to the city of Calgary for the famous Calgary Stampede. Top of the bill is the **rodeo**, with events such as riding a bucking bronco and bull wrestling. Yikes!

From timber to apple trees

Posted by: Ben Blog | 3 January at 10.53 a.m.

Back in British Columbia, we called in on this giant sawmill. It is where logs are cut into smaller pieces of wood. More than half of Canada is covered in forests, and wood is very important. The wood and wood products, such as paper, are sold all over the world.

BARKO'S BLOG-TASTIC CANADA FACTS

Fancy a crunchy apple? Farmers in Canada grow apples in large **orchards** along the shores of Lakes Ontario, Erie and Huron. They also grow grapes, blueberries, peaches, plums, cranberries and pears.

And finally ...

Posted by: Ben Blog | 14 February at 8.12 a.m.

Our last stop was Niagara Falls, three whopping waterfalls on the border between Canada and the United States. This is Horseshoe Falls on the Canadian side. Here, the water falls around 53 metres (173 feet). You can watch it land from a tunnel near the bottom. What a splash!

BARKO'S BLOG-TASTIC CANADA FACTS

This is Banff National Park in the Rocky Mountains. It's a stunning place, with ice-capped mountains, **glaciers**, lakes and forests. It's also home to some amazing animals, including **caribou**, wolves and grizzly bears, such as this one.

Canada fact file

Area: 9,984,670 square kilometres
(3,855,103 square miles)

Population: 35,427,524 (2014)

Capital city: Ottawa

Other main cities: Toronto, Montreal, Vancouver

Languages: English, French

Main religion: Christianity

Highest mountain: Mount Logan
(5,959 metres/19,551 feet)

Longest river: Mackenzie River
(1,650 kilometres/1,025 miles)

Currency: Canadian dollar

Canada quiz

Find out how much you know about Canada with our quick quiz.

1. Which country does Canada join on to?
a) Greenland
b) United States
c) Russia

2. Which is the world's biggest lake?
a) Lake Erie
b) Lake Huron
c) Lake Superior

3. What is maple syrup made from?
a) maple tree **sap**
b) maple tree leaves
c) maple tree bark

4. Where is ice hockey played?
a) on a field
b) on a track
c) on a rink

5. What is this?

27

Glossary

aerobatic spectacular flight by a group of aeroplanes

caribou large North American reindeer

descended from related to people from a long time ago

glacier river of ice that flows from a mountain or sheet of ice

inquisitive interested in learning about the world

Inuit people who have lived in the Arctic for thousands of years

Marco Polo explorer who lived from about 1254 to 1324. He travelled from Italy to China.

orchard places where fruit trees are grown

rodeo display of horse-riding skills and rounding up cattle

sap thick, sticky substance under the bark of a tree

scavenge search for something among rubbish

Viking people who lived in Scandinavia about 1,000 years ago

Find out more

Books

Canada (Countries Around the World), Michael Hurley (Raintree, 2012)

The Kids Book of Canada, Barbara Greenwood (Kids Can Press, 2007)

Websites

www.kids-world-travel-guide.com/canada-facts. html
This website contains interesting Australia facts that have been chosen and researched by children especially for other children.

www.kids.nationalgeographic.co.uk/kids/ places/find
National Geographic's website has lots of information, photos and maps of countries around the world.

www.worldatlas.com
Packed with information about different countries, this website has flags, time zones, facts and figures, maps and timelines.

Index